NIKALAS CATLOW & TIM WESSON
AWESOMELY BRILLIANT DOODLES
PIRATES VS DINOSAURS
SCHOLASTIC
AF378716

Scholastic Children's Books,
Euston House,
24 Eversholt Street,
London NW1 1DB, UK

A division of Scholastic Ltd
London ~ New York ~ Toronto ~ Sydney ~ Auckland
Mexico City ~ New Delhi ~ Hong Kong

Editor: Elizabeth Scoggins

Published in the UK by Scholastic Ltd, 2013
Text and illustrations by Nikalas Catlow and Tim Wesson
Text and illustrations © Nikalas Catlow and dogonarock (uk) Ltd, 2013

The material in this book previously appeared in
Seriously Silly Activities: Pirates, published 2010, and
Seriously Silly Activities: Dinosaurs, published 2010.

ISBN 978 1407 13740 7

Printed and bound by Bell & Bain Ltd, United Kingdom

WARNING!

This book might be too awesomely brilliant for your brain!

Bad Bob Big-Pants

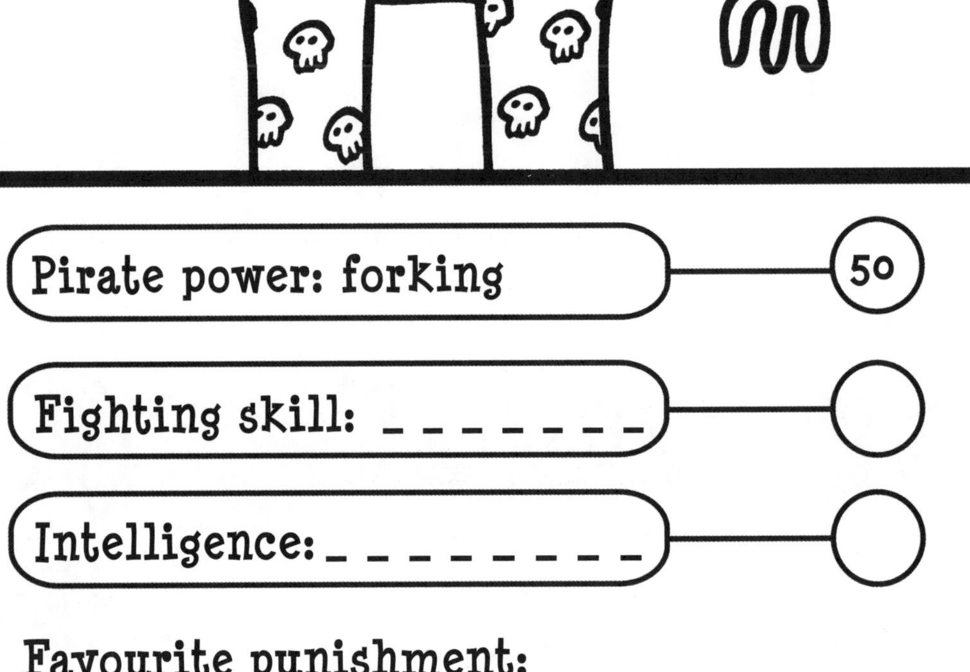

Hulk-o-don

Special power: pounding — 80

Fighting skill: _ _ _ _ _ _ _

Intelligence:_ _ _ _ _ _ _ _

Favourite punishment: _ _ _ _ _ _ _ _ _

_ _ _ _ _ _ _ _ _ _ _ _ _ _ _ _

How to draw a pirate

3

4

The fight!
How many pirates can you see?
Colour them in!

Give US skin!
Create dinosaur skin texture any way you like.
I'm covered with dots and scales!
HB

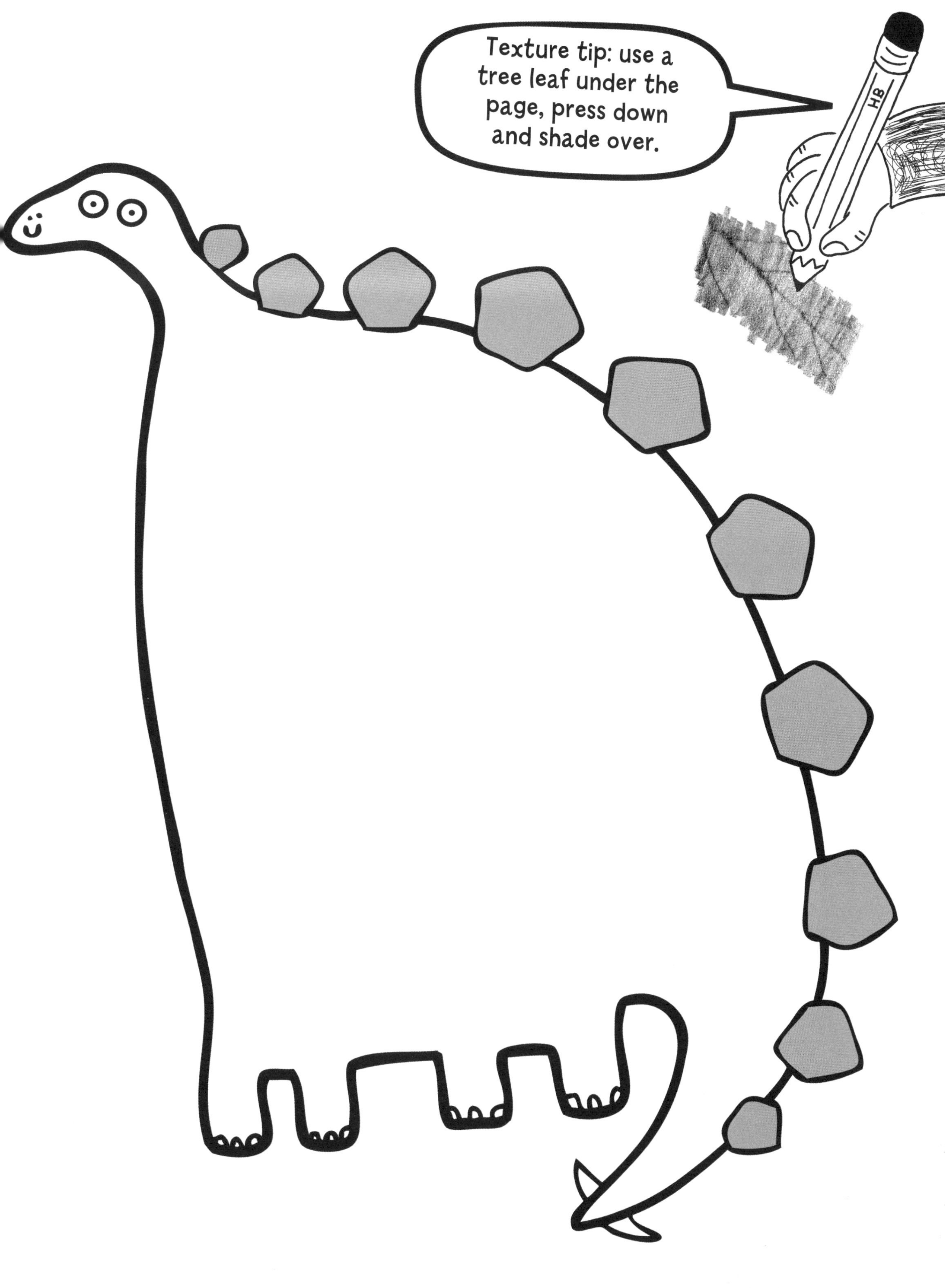

Texture tip: use a tree leaf under the page, press down and shade over.
HB

Finish the crew

Give them silly heads and stupid bodies!

Make your own treasure map

Draw a dotted line for the journey from the ship to the treasure. Add some obstacles and booby traps along the way.

Add some brilliant place names!
ARRR! Mark an 'X' where the treasure is buried.

Booty Spotter!

Draw
Bad Bob
Big-Pants
We've started
you off with
his outline.

Give u
scaly
skin.
Dinosaur
SPOt!
How many dinosaurs
can you see?
Colour me!

Eyes here!

Name: Tap-Dancing Terry

Dance skills:

Height:

Weight:

Shoe size:

Ambition:

Name: Fat Fred Furry-Face

Dance skills:

Height:

Weight:

Shoe size:

Ambition:

Treasure
maze
START

Find the buried treasure chest, and pick up any booty you find on the way!

Greedy Bob

YOU write the story.

Grow your own dinosaur

Create your own
dinosaur in a pot!

Draw your own dinosaur in four easy steps!

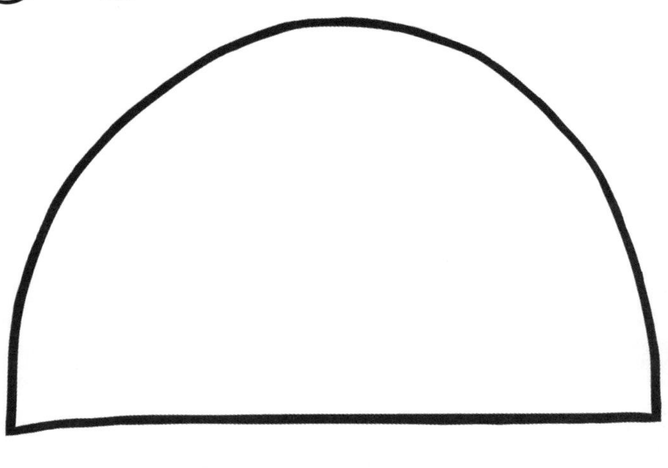

1.

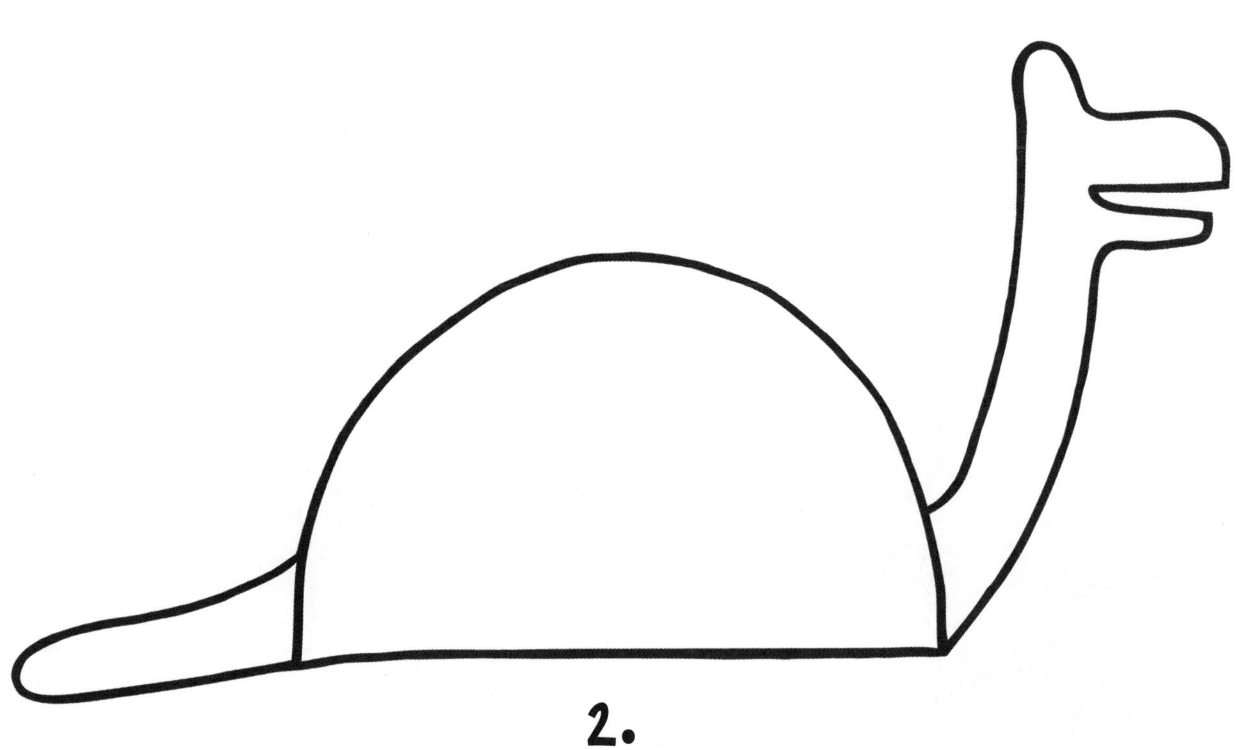

2.

3.
Ta-da!
4.

Leglessaurus and...

...Scurvy dog sea legs

Feed the sea monster

I'll eat anything!
AAAA

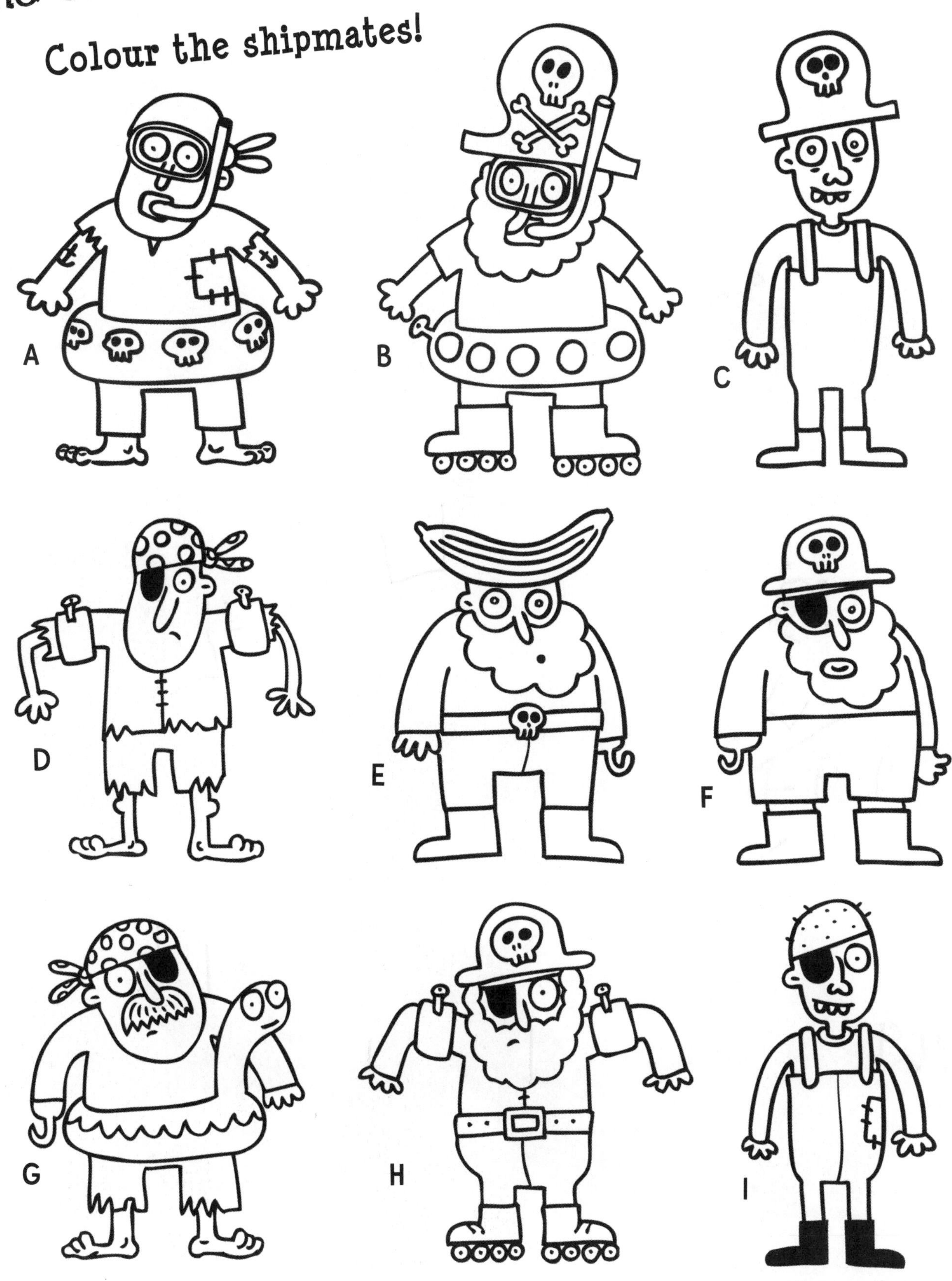

The crew of the Barmy Barnacle
Colour the shipmates!
A
B
C
D
E
F
G
H
I

Match the crew to their shadows!

Shiver me timbers!
What orders is the captain shouting?

WIEP YOUR BUM WITH A STIK!!
POO IN YOUR GRANDADS MEE T BALES!!
Give me something to do, Cap'n, arrr!

Surf to safety
or burn out!
START
Lava-
surfing
maze

Finish!

Robo-raptor

Dinosaur Skill: x-ray vision — 85

Fighting Skill:

Strength:

Parrot-Brain Joe

Pirate Skill: bird-brainy — 80

Fighting Skill:

Strength:

Create your own...

pirate flags

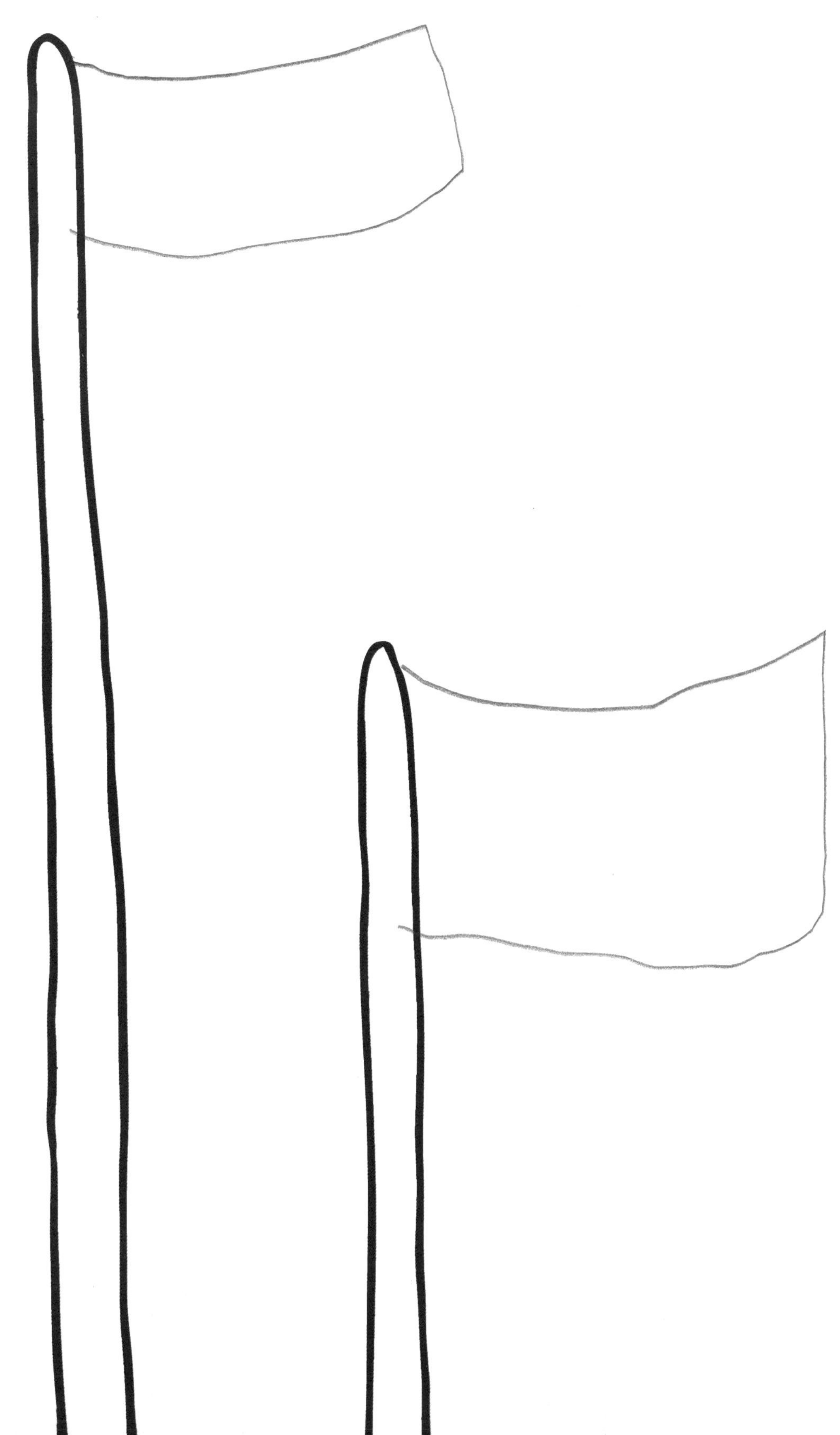

Create your own hooks!

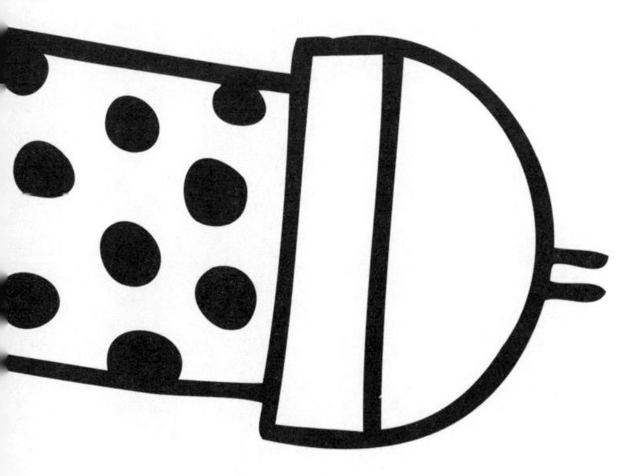

Buried treasure

Fill the hole with booty!

Create your own
pirate parrot.

Shape-o-saurs

Create dinosaurs using circles, squares, rectangles and triangles!

Dinodoku
Chomp! Chomp!

		3	
	4		
		1	
	2		

Fill in the squares so that every row, column and 2 x 2 box contains the numbers 1, 2, 3 and 4.

Draw Super-Saurus
My left side is my best side...
We've started you off with his outline... Fill in the rest!

Digestive maze

Piratoku

2
1
2
4
3

Fill in the squares so that every row, column and 2 x 2 box contains the numbers 1, 2, 3 and 4. Arrrr, my head hurts!

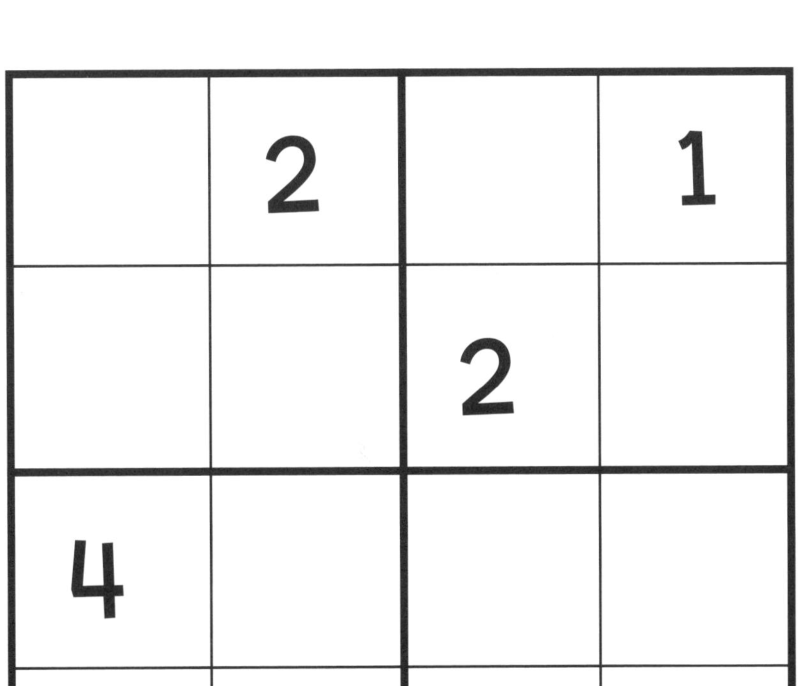

Pirate wordbot

Dotty dino

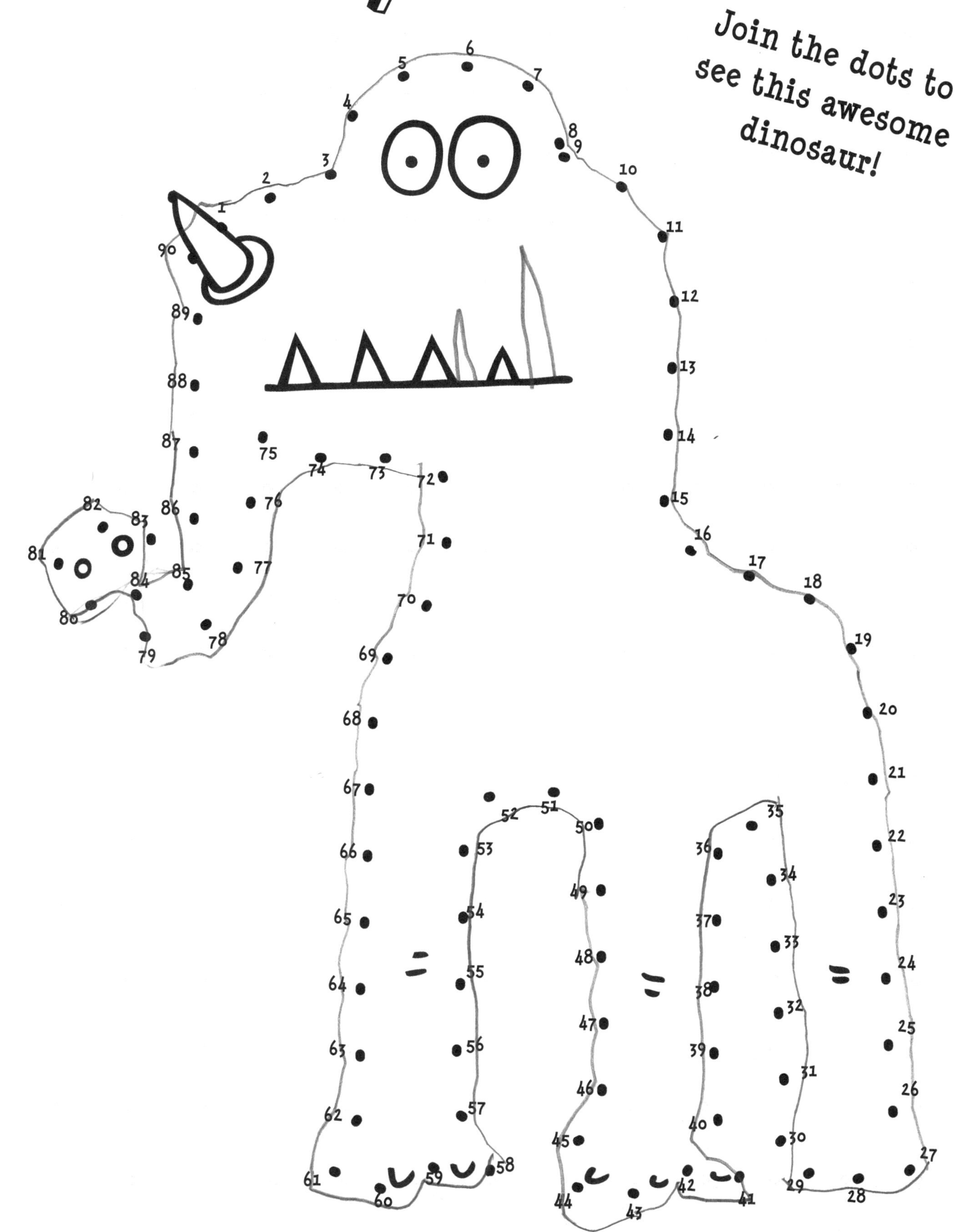

WOUld You rather
be smashed by a
Brontosaurus...  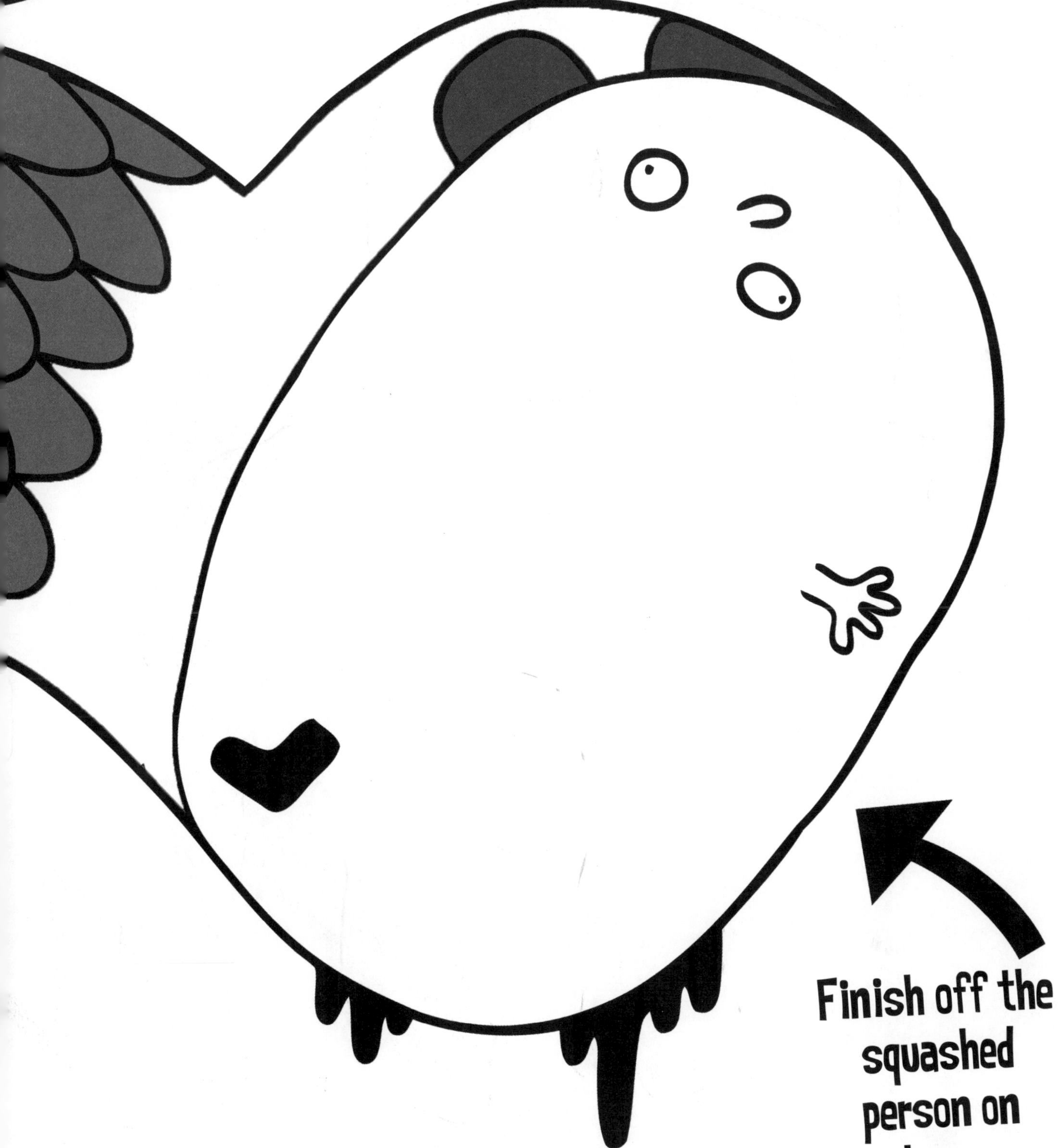
Finish off the
squashed
person on
here.

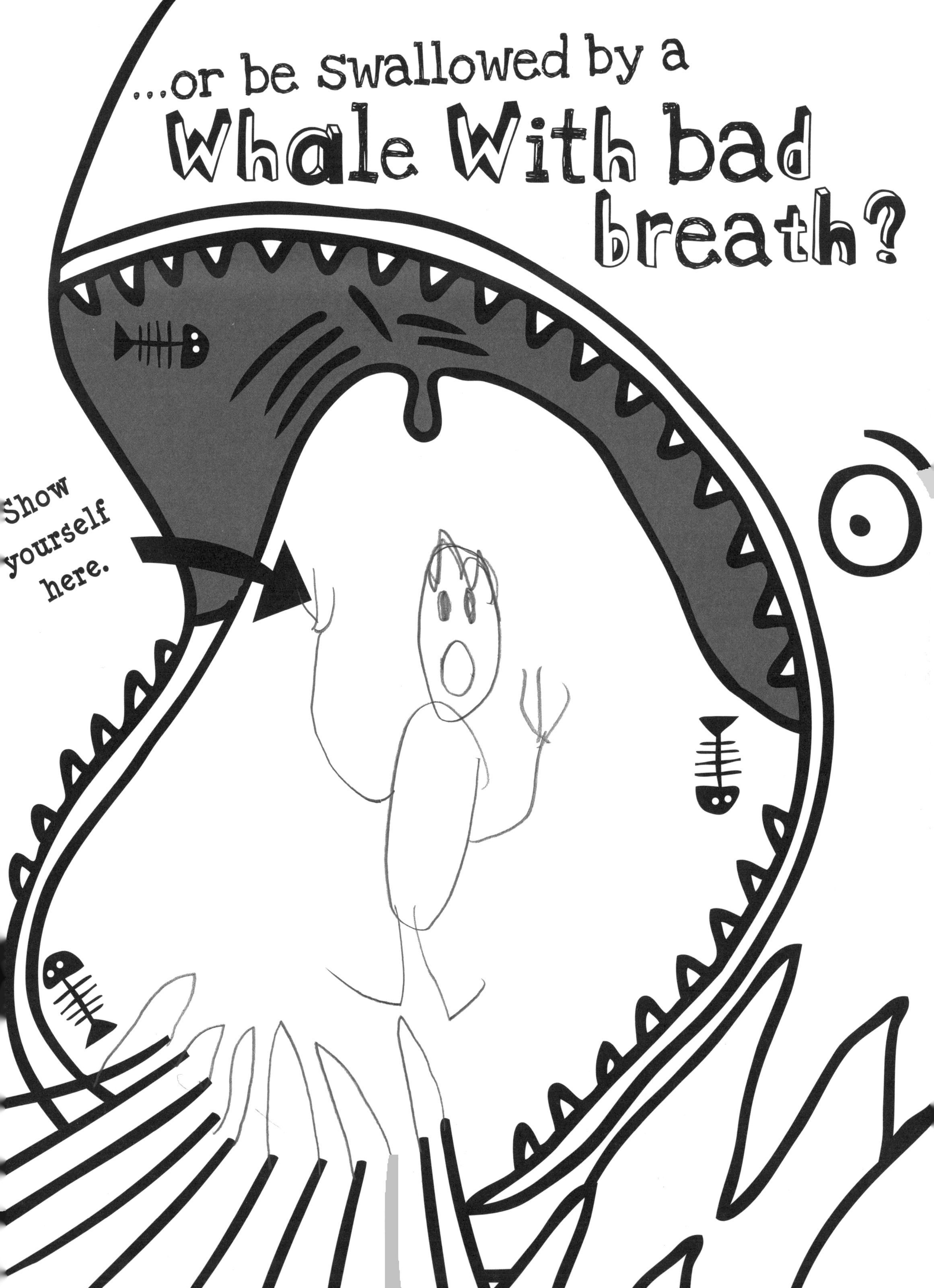
...or be swallowed by a
Whale With bad breath?
Show yourself here.

Pirate luggage mix-up

Captain Crab is ready to set sail. Before he goes, help him match his luggage with its contents.

Up the anchor,
me hearties!
Hoist the main sail,
steady as she goes!

Give their clothes
spots...

...OR stripes.

Design-O-saurs
Evolve your own!

Igu-MAN-odon

Here are 3 ideas!
1. Tyrannus-CAT
2. Diplo-DOG-us
3. Ptero-CACTUS

Who's better?
You decide!
Pete Peg
V
Pirate power: hammering
80
Fighting skill: _ _ _ _ _ _ _ _
Strength: _ _ _ _ _ _ _ _ _ _
Favourite punishment: _ _ _ _ _ _ _ _ _
_ _ _ _ _ _ _ _ _ _ _ _ _ _ _ _ _

Parrot-Brain Joe

Dinosaur power: wizardry — 85

Fighting skill: _ _ _ _ _ _ _

Strength: _ _ _ _ _ _ _ _ _ _

Favourite punishment: _ _ _ _ _ _ _ _ _

_ _ _ _ _ _ _ _ _ _ _ _ _ _ _ _ _ _ _

Awesome answers

The fight!

There are 17 pirates fighting

Booty spotter

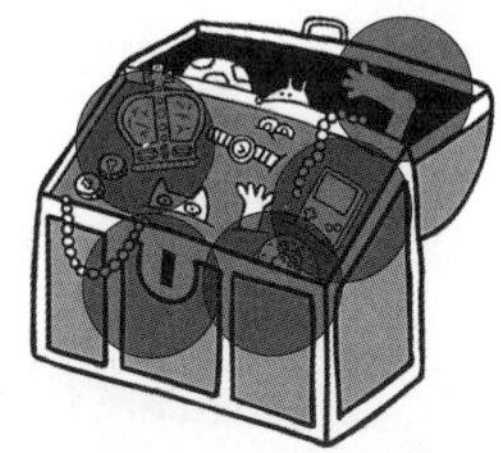

Dinosaur spot!

There are 18 crazy dinosaurs

Treasure maze

The crew of the Barmy Barnacle

A:6, B:5, C:4, D:7, E:8, F:1, G:9, H:2, I:3

Lava-surfing maze

Dinodoku

2	1	3	4
3	4	2	1
4	3	1	2
1	2	4	3

Digestion maze

Piratoku

3	2	4	1
1	4	2	3
4	1	3	2
2	3	1	4

Pirate wordbot

h	u	l	e	v	e	r	n
a		b	a	t	t	e	r	y
m	e	l	b	n	e	q	p
m	t	s	n	t	g	t	s
e	b	a	u	y	c	l	e
r	p	o	i	l	c	a	n
s	m	o	u	s	e	p	g
n	u	t	c	c	h	i	p

Pirate luggage mix-up

A:6, B:3, C:8, D:1, E:5, F:9, G:7, H:4, I:2